Little Pebble™

Our Amazing Senses

Our Ears Can Hear

T0052421

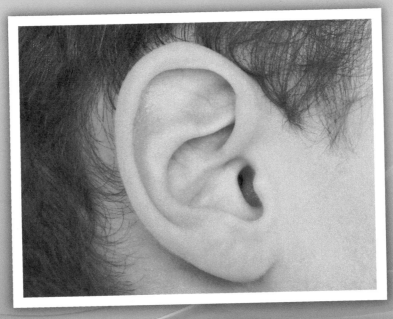

by Jodi-Wheeler Toppen

CAPSTONE PRESS
a capstone imprint

Little Pebble is published by Capstone Press,
1710 Roe Crest Drive, North Mankato, Minnesota 56003
www.mycapstone.com

Library of Congress Cataloging-in-Publication Data
Names: Wheeler-Toppen, Jodi, author.
Title: Our ears can hear / by Jodi-Wheeler Toppen.
Description: North Mankato, Minnesota : Capstone Press, [2018] | Series: Our
  amazing sense | Audience: Age 4-7. | Audience: K to grade 3. | Includes
  bibliographical references and index.
Identifiers: LCCN 2017005235 (print) | LCCN 2017006586 (ebook)
ISBN 9781515767138 (library binding)
ISBN 9781515767183 (paperback)
ISBN 9781515767237 (eBook PDF)
Subjects: LCSH: Hearing—Juvenile literature. | Ear—Juvenile literature. |
  Senses and sensation—Juvenile literature.
Classification: LCC QP462.2 .W44 2018 (print) | LCC QP462.2 (ebook) | DDC
  612.8/5—dc23
LC record available at https://lccn.loc.gov/2017005235

Editorial Credits
Abby Colich, editor; Juliette Peters, designer; Wanda Winch, media researcher;
Tori Abraham, production specialist

Photo Credits
Shutterstock: agsandrew, motion design element, AJP, 17, Alexander_P, 13, Bernatskaya
Oxana, 1, ESB Professional, 21, fotographic1980, sound wave design, naluwan, cover,
nattapan72, 9, Oscity, 5, Reddogs, 19, Robert Kneschke, 11, wavebreakmedia, 7, xrender,
15

Printed in the United States   5692

Table of Contents

It's Sound!. 4

Sound Moves 8

Glossary. 22
Read More. 23
Internet Sites 23
Critical Thinking Questions 24
Index. 24

It's Sound!

Ding! Honk!

Bang! Beep!

Sound is all around you.

Boom! Thud!

Ears hear loud noise.

Shh...

Ears hear quiet
sounds too.

Sound Moves

Toss a rock in a pond.

Splash!

Hear it land.

See the waves?

That's how sound moves.

It moves in waves.

sound wave

Sound waves go in your ear.

They hit your eardrum.

They tap tiny bones.

Tap. Tap. Tap.

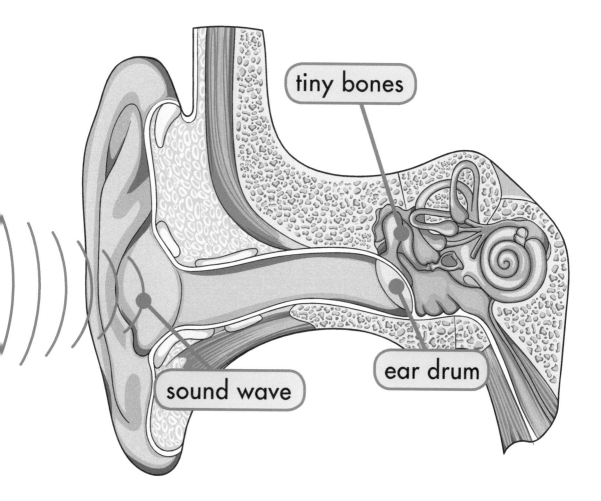

tiny bones

sound wave

ear drum

Sound hits the inner ear.

Tiny hairs shake.

The hairs are stuck to cells.

sound wave

hair

cell

The cells send a signal.

Your brain gets a message.

It knows the sound.

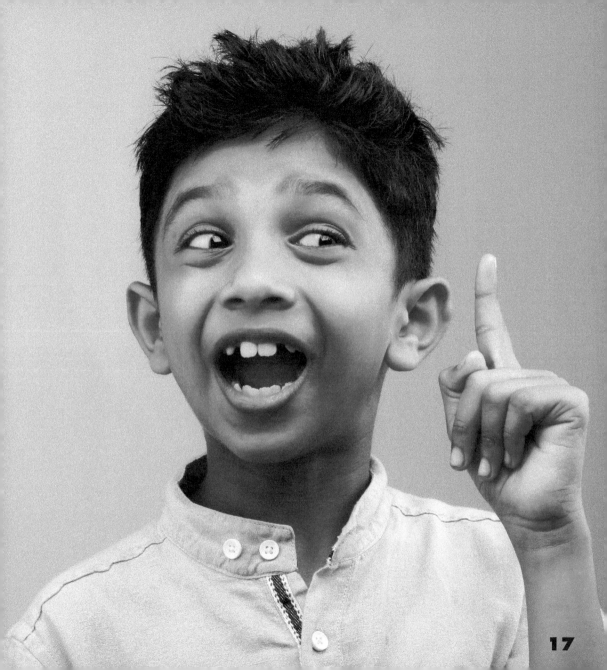

Listen.

Woof. Woof.

Spot barks.

Where is he?

Look! There's Spot!

Your ears can hear.

They help you find

the sound.

Glossary

brain—the organ inside your head that controls your movements, thoughts, and feelings

cell—the smallest unit of a living thing

eardrum—a thin piece of skin stretched tight like a drum inside the ear

inner ear—part of ear farthest inside the head; the inner ear is in charge of hearing and balance

wave—the energy moving through air or water

Read More

Appleby, Alex. *What I Hear.* My Five Senses. New York: Gareth Stevens Publishing, 2015.

Murray, Julie. *I Can Hear.* Senses. Minneapolis, Minn.: Abdo Kids, 2016.

Rustad, Martha E.H. *Hearing.* Senses in My World. Minneapolis, Minn.: Bullfrog Books, 2015.

Internet Sites

Use FactHound to find Internet sites related to this book.

Visit *www.facthound.com*
Type in this code: 9781515767138

Super-cool stuff!

Check out projects, games and lots more at
www.capstonekids.com

Critical Thinking Questions

1. Name two parts that are inside your ear.

2. The text says that sound moves through the air in waves. Use the glossary on page 22 to define the word *wave*.

Index

bones, 12

brains, 16

cells, 14, 16

eardrums, 12

ears, 6, 12, 20

hairs, 14

inner ears, 14

sounds, 4, 6, 10, 14, 16, 20

sound waves, 10, 12